IDANRE AND OTHER POEMS

The Guardian

Wole Soyinka is an internationally known playwright. He has had plays produced in London and New York. In 1966–1967 he received a British Arts Council John Whiting Award for his work as a playwright. Formerly Director of the Drama School at Ibadan University, Nigeria, he is presently in jail in his native country for allegedly supporting secessionist Biafra.

IDANRE

& OTHER
POEMS
BY
WOLE
SOYINKA

HILL AND WANG / NEW YORK

FIRST PUBLISHED IN 1967 BY METHUEN & CO. LTD
© WOLE SOYINKA 1967
ALL RIGHTS RESERVED
PUBLISHED IN THE UNITED STATES OF AMERICA
BY HILL AND WANG, INC.
STANDARD BOOK NUMBER (CLOTHBOUND EDITION): 8090-5725-5
STANDARD BOOK NUMBER (PAPERBACK EDITION): 8090-1352-5
LIBRARY OF CONGRESS CATALOG CARD NUMBER: 68-30761
FIRST AMERICAN EDITION SEPTEMBER 1968

SECOND PRINTING (FIRST HILL AND WANG
PAPERBACK EDITION) AUGUST 1969
PRINTED IN THE UNITED STATES OF AMERICA
234567890

CONTENTS

Such webs as these we build our dreams upon
To quiver lightly and to fly
The sun comes down in stately visit
The spider feeds him pearls.

of the road

DAWN

Breaking earth upon
A spring-haired elbow, lone
A palm beyond head-grains, spikes
A guard of prim fronds, piercing
High hairs of the wind

As one who bore the pollen highest

Blood-drops in the air, above
The even belt of tassels, above
Coarse leaf teasing on the waist, steals
The lone intruder, tearing wide

The chaste hide of the sky

O celebration of the rites of dawn
Night-spread in tatters and a god
Received, aflame with kernels.

DEATH IN THE DAWN

Driving to Lagos one morning a white cockerel flew out of the dusk and smashed itself against my windscreen. A mile further I came across a motor accident and a freshly dead man in the smash.

Traveller, you must set out
At dawn. And wipe your feet upon
The dog-nose wetness of earth.

Let sunrise quench your lamps, and watch
Faint brush pricklings in the sky light
Cottoned feet to break the early earthworm
On the hoe. Now shadows stretch with sap
Not twilight's death and sad prostration

This soft kindling, soft receding breeds
Racing joys and apprehensions for
A naked day, burdened hulks retract,
Stoop to the mist in faceless throng
To wake the silent markets – swift, mute
Processions on grey byways. . . .

On this
Counterpane, it was –
Sudden winter at the death
Of dawn's lone trumpeter, cascades
Of white feather-flakes, but it proved
A futile rite. Propitiation sped
Grimly on, before.

The right foot for joy, the left, dread
And the mother prayed, Child
May you never walk
When the road waits, famished.

Traveller you must set forth
At dawn
I promise marvels of the holy hour
Presages as the white cock's flapped
Perverse impalement – as who would dare
The wrathful wings of man's Progression. . . .

But such another Wraith! Brother,
Silenced in the startled hug of
Your invention – is this mocked grimace
This closed contortion – I?

AROUND US, DAWNING

Jet flight

This beast was fashioned well; it prowls
The rare selective heights
And spurns companionship with bird

Wings are tipped in sulphurs
Scouring grey recesses of the void
To a linear flare of dawns

Red haloes through the ports wreathe us
Passive martyrs, bound to a will of rotors

Yielding ours,
To the alien mote
The hidden ache . . . when
Death makes a swift descent

The mountains range in spire on spire
Lances at the bold carbuncle
On the still night air. I am light honed

To a still point in the incandescent
Onrush, a fine ash in the beast's sudden
Dessication when the sun explodes.

LUO PLAINS

Kenya

Plague
Of comet tails, of bled horizons
Where egrets hone a sky-lane for
Worlds to turn on pennants

Lakemists
On her shadeless dugs, parched
At waterhole. Veils. Molten silver
Down cloudflues of alchemist sun . . .
A lake's grey salve at dawn?

That dawn
Her eyes were tipped with sunset spears
Seasons' quills upon her parchment, yet
The hidden lake of her

Forgives!

For she has milked a cycle of
Red sunset spears, sucked reeds of poison
To a cowherd's flute. The plains
Are swift again on migrant wings
And the cactus
Flowers the eagle sentinel.

IN MEMORY OF SEGUN AWOLOWO

For him who was
Lifted on tar sprays
And gravel rains

In metallic timbres
Harder than milestone heart

For him who was.

The road, the aged road
Retched on this fresh plunder
Of my youth

An error of the sun
A mirage upon earth's
Apostate face

For him who fell among reapers
Who forestall the harvest

And drove
The last flint deepest
In the heart of patience

Death the scrap-iron dealer
Breeds a glut on trade. The fault
Is His of seven paths whose whim
Gave Death his agency

In sounds as of the river's
Failing pulse, of shifting earth
They make complaint

Grey presences of head and hands
Who wander still
Adrift from understanding.

lone figure

THE DREAMER

Higher than trees a cryptic crown
Lord of the rebel three
Thorns lay on a sleep of down
And myrrh; a mesh
Of nails, of flesh
And words that flowered free

A cleft between the birches
Next year is reaping time
The fruit will fall to searchers
Cleansed of mould
Chronicles of gold
Mourn a fruit in prime.

The burden bowed the boughs to earth
A girdle for the see
And bitter pods gave voices birth
A ring of stones
And throes and thrones
And incense on the sea.

THE HUNCHBACK OF DUGBE

I wondered always where
He walked at night, or lay
Where earth might seem
Suddenly in labour when he sighed.

By day, stooped at public drains
Intense at bath or washing cotton holes,
An ant's blown load upon
A child's entangled scrawl

The calmest nudist
Of the roadside lunatics.

The devil came one sane night
On parole from hell, lace curtains
Sieved light dancing pebbles
On his vast creation egg

His cement mixer borne
On crossed cassava sticks.

Not in disdain, but in truth immune
From song or terror, taxi turns
And sale fuss of the mad, beyond
Ugliness or beauty, whom thought-sealing

Solemnly transfigures – the world
Spins on his spine, in still illusion.

But the bell-tower of his thin
Buttocks rings pure tones on Dugbe
A horse penis loin to crooked knees
Side-slapping on his thighs

At night he prowls, a cask
Of silence; on his lone matrix
Pigeon eggs of light dance in and out
Of dark, and he walks in motley.

THE LAST LAMP

A pale
Incision in the skin of night
It dwindled downhill, weaker bled
From pole to passage, dye
And shroud

Her shadow
Now indrawn from dances
On the silent eaves
Gathers close about her –
A lying depth

Oil is a kindly lamp
To generations' patient stoop
In crooked doorways, to a market's
Final breath

Of patience, peace denied . . .
She was a vespers' valediction, lit
Within deserted ribs.

EASTER

This slow day dies, a wordless wilt
Shades of silence reaping
Soft frangipanes

Pollen's wings are thorned; bosoms
Too welcoming fold later chills
Take death to innocents

Kinder these hard mangoes, greendrops
At the ear of god-apparent, coquettes
To the future decadence.

Do we not truly fear to bleed? We hunt
Pale tissues of the palm, fingers groping
Ever cautious on the crown.

These pink frangipanes of Easter crop
Eager to the wind; by repetition weak
And rain's in-breeding,

One bough to slake the millions? Decay
Caulks earth's centre; spurned we pluck
Bleached petals for the dreamer's lair.

Borne passive on this gift, wound-splashes
From wind scavenger, sap fragrance for
A heady brew, I rode my winged ass and raged –

As children wove frond yellow from the palm
Plucked at the core, within the spadix heart.

of birth and death

KOKO OLORO

From a children's propitiation chant

Dolorous kno
Plead for me
Farm or hill
Plead for me
Stream and wind
Take my voice
Home or road
Plead for me
On this shoot, I
Bind your leaves
Stalk and bud
Berries three
On the threshold
Cast my voice
Knot of bitters
Plead for me.

DEDICATION

For Moremi, 1963

Earth will not share the rafter's envy: dung floors
Break, not the gecko's slight skin, but its fall
Taste this soil for death and plumb her deep for life

As this yam, wholly earthed, yet a living tuber
To the warmth of waters, earthed as springs
As roots of baobab, as the hearth.

The air will not deny you. Like a top
Spin you on the navel of the storm, for the hoe
That roots the forests ploughs a path for squirrels.

Be ageless as dark peat, but only that rain's
Fingers, not the feet of men may wash you over.
Long wear the sun's shadow; run naked to the night.

Peppers green and red – child – your tongue arch
To scorpion tail, spit straight return to danger's threats
Yet coo with the brown pigeon, tendril dew between your lips.

Shield you like the flesh of palms, skyward held
Cuspids in thorn nesting, insealed as the heart of kernel –
A woman's flesh is oil – child, palm oil on your tongue

Is suppleness to life, and wine of this gourd
From self-same timeless run of runnels as refill
Your podlings, child, weaned from yours we embrace

Earth's honeyed milk, wine of the only rib.
Now roll your tongue in honey till your cheeks are
Swarming honeycombs – your world needs sweetening, child.

Camwood round the heart, chalk for flight
Of blemish – see? it dawns! – antimony beneath
Armpits like a goddess, and leave this taste

Long on your lips, of salt, that you may seek
None from tears. This, rain-water, is the gift
Of gods – drink of its purity, bear fruits in season.

Fruits then to your lips: haste to repay
The debt of birth. Yield man-tides like the sea
And ebbing, leave a meaning on the fossilled sands.

A CRY IN THE NIGHT

Burial of a still-born

> As who would break
> Earth, grief
> In savage pounding, moulds
> Her forehead where she kneels.
>
> No stars caress her keening
> The sky recedes from pain
>
> Nor will this night dark
> Shield her. Defiance falls back
> Barren, heaven may not contest
> Scars, shower ancient scales
> To prove her torment shared.

[25]

Such tender stalk is earthed
In haste. A stricken snake, she drags
Across the gulf, re-enters to the retch
Of grieving wombs. Night harshly folds her
Broken as her afterbirth.

A FIRST DEATHDAY

We triumphed then upon the wails of birth
And felt no fears. By mute assertion
Of the later year, she marked *her* victory
Grief has long receded, yet the wonder
Stays.

Truly, it was a deed of grace, this death
At the first teething, contrary
Precision of her first birthday, almost
On the hour.

Knowledge as this in growth's diffusion
Thins, till shrouds are torn from swaddlings.
She was not one more veil, dark across
The Secret; Folasade ran bridal to the Spouse
Wise to fore-planning – bear witness, Time
To my young will, in this last breath
Of mockery.

FOR THE PIPER DAUGHTERS (1960)

Seeking – as who has not? – beauty
Lodged in concaves of the yielded;
Conniving lies with self-encrimsoned mists,
Your laugh
        Meant,
Your warmth,
        Given,
And innocence
        Lightly
As your next footfall – unpractised,
Left after right – this, your revelation
Unmasks past seemings.

I would not have you cruel, nor change
Your largesse for the slits
In hoarded goodness – yet
To the date
        A stone
The linnet
        Height
Pearls
        Depth and the clam;
The rose, you know, is thorned. And if
The cozening priest would slay you, panting
How your cheeks are rudded like the . . . !
Riddle him with lethal pips!

I would not have you age. I swear
I would not have you filter
Dust in the sun, unless you – like the wind –
               Will dance
The tree
               Pray
Pebbles
               Chant
Night
Dance glad anguish of the mother rites,
Unravel seeds, the stranger essence
Sprung from your goodness. I would you
Thus, never never old.

ABIKU

*Wanderer child. It is the same child who dies and returns again and
again to plague the mother – Yoruba belief.*

In vain your bangles cast
Charmed circles at my feet
I am Abiku, calling for the first
And the repeated time.

Must I weep for goats and cowries
For palm oil and the sprinkled ash?
Yams do not sprout in amulets
To earth Abiku's limbs.

So when the snail is burnt in his shell,
Whet the heated fragment, brand me
Deeply on the breast – you must know him
When Abiku calls again.

I am the squirrel teeth, cracked
The riddle of the palm; remember
This, and dig me deeper still into
The god's swollen foot.

Once and the repeated time, ageless
Though I puke, and when you pour
Libations, each finger points me near
The way I came, where

The ground is wet with mourning
White dew suckles flesh-birds
Evening befriends the spider, trapping
Flies in wine-froth;

Night, and Abiku sucks the oil
From lamps. Mothers! I'll be the
Suppliant snake coiled on the doorstep
Yours the killing cry.

The ripest fruit was saddest;
Where I crept, the warmth was cloying.
In silence of webs, Abiku moans, shaping
Mounds from the yolk.

TO MY FIRST WHITE HAIRS

Hirsute hell chimney-spouts, black thunderthroes
confluence of coarse cloudfleeces – my head sir! – scourbrush
in bitumen, past fossil beyond fingers of light – until . . . !

Sudden sprung as corn stalk after rain, watered milk weak;
as lightning shrunk to ant's antenna, shrivelled
off the febrile sight of crickets in the sun –

THREE WHITE HAIRS! frail invaders of the undergrowth
interpret time. I view them, wired wisps, vibrant coiled
beneath a magnifying glass, milk-thread presages

Of the hoary phase. Weave then, weave o quickly weave
your sham veneration. Knit me webs of winter sagehood,
nightcap, and the fungoid sequins of a crown.

[30]

there are more functions to a freezing plant
than stocking beer; cold biers of mortuaries
submit their dues, harnessed – glory be! –

is the cold hand of death . . .
his mouth was cotton filled, his man-pike
shrunk to sub-soil grub

his head was hollowed and his brain
on scales – was this a trick to prove
fore-knowledge after death?

his flesh confesses what has stilled
his tongue; masked fingers think from him
to learn, how not to die.

let us love all things of grey; grey slabs
grey scalpel, one grey sleep and form,
grey images.

for women

SONG: DESERTED MARKETS

To a Paris night

Deserted markets
Runnels of rain
Seeds fill your gutters
And a long night of pain.

Let me stammer my life
Down your endless lane
The night is for dreaming
And a long bed of pain.

My soul shall be dry
In an ebony grain
Keep it from sprouting
In a stranger's pain.

A night for a life
Dawn hastens in vain
A white bird she comes
And gobbles the grain

For night flowed between
Moon-breasts of pain
And the dew leaves no mark
Where my head has lain.

PSALM

the seeds have ripened fast my love
and the milk is straining at the pods

the ever-eager thought is chaste
at the ruin of your corn-stalk waist

swaddlings of my gratitude
stir within your plenitude.

moist the quickening consciousness
sealed in warm mis-shapenness

ivory granaries are filled
a prize of pain will be fulfilled

bright stream from unbroken springs
threads of ever linking rings

sealed in earth your sanctuary
yields to light; and a mystery

     of pulses and the stranger life
     comes to harvest and release
     the germ and life exegesis
     inspiration of your genesis.

HER JOY IS WILD

Her joy is wild, wild
Wave-breaking she proclaims,
Your strong teeth will weaken
If you nibble the rind.

Her strength is wild, wild
Wild as the love that sings –
This is the last-born; give me
A joyful womb to bind.

The hour is wild, wild
Denies the wispy moments. Yet
When the fist is loosened, when
The knot is cut, you'll find

Skeins of hair. Wild, wild
Her laughter, dreaming that the tribe
Had slain the senile chieftain
That the rite – was kind.

Her words are wild, wild
Shell the future, place the nut
Between my teeth – and I denied her
Nothing, maimed on her vision of the blind.

BLACK SINGER

(for Marge, New York)

Cold wreath of vine, darkly
Coiled about the night; echoes deep within
Bled veins of autumn

A votive vase, her throat
Poured many souls as one; how dark
The wine became the night.

Fleshed from out disjointed, out from
The sidewalk hurt of sirens, a darkling
Pool of wine shivers

In light shrapnels, and do you ask
How *is* the wine tonight? Dark, lady
Dark in token of the deeper wounds

Full again of promises
Of the deep and silent wounds
Of cruel phases of the darksome wine

Song, O Voice, is lonely envoy
Night a runnel for the wine's indifferent flow.

BRINGER OF PEACE

You come as light rain not to quench
But question out the pride of fire
Watchlight to my peace, within and out
Unguarded moments and the human hours.

You come as light rain, swift to soothe
The rent in earth with deft intrusion
To test your peace on a hiss of ashes
Your sky of lakes on thirsts of embers

Yet fires that hold the beast at bay
Inclose, with all accomplishments of rage
The inborn howl, proud lacerations
Futile vaults at high bounds of the pit

This cunning sift of mild aggression, then
Is your rain, a tacit lie of stillness
A smile to test the python's throes, a touch
To bring the bowstring's nerve to rest.

TO ONE, IN LABOUR

For Segi

In silent spaces of the firebrush
Mud regurgitations of the ant
Break air and pollen grain.
The architects

Of spathe and spire survive
Subversions of the human tread
Or mind, some to labour some to yield
A queen her labour

But they build. And I think
Gestation is a Queen insealed
In the cathedral heart, dead lovers round
Her nave of life.

Departed now, the master masons. Desolate
Wonder of you and me, mud spires
Thrust inviolate against colonnades
Of heartwood. Within,

A Queen preparing. Alas for dead lovers
And the silent shrine of pain. In solitude
Of catacombs the lethal arc contracts, my love –
Of your secretions.

[38]

IN PATHS OF RAIN

In paths of rain, in rock grooves, may
These rare instants of wild fox-fires
Write on moments, lives.

The moment's lightning felt
On wire-tips, as fire-surrounds
To heartbeat of a trembling hare

The last despairing pause, birth-teasing
Yields dues on precipice, to love,
Reassurance, and strangled seeds

Unleashed, exult. From wells
Deep in the brute's denials comes
A captive tenderness

Shy lights from your night redress
My darkness, sable oil still-traps
A straining thunderhead

In unguent silt to rest
Roots of rage held to a lucent stance
Glow-swarms lightening

High thorn-bushes. Clean vistas –
Flecked mica after rain, plankton in antimony
Off rain-washed shores.

[39]

Till the chronicle of severance,
Gold spelling, lantern sanctuaries around
Birth-point, and chapter. . . .

Ground skins of the unshelled
                              hand over hand of fire
A kernel's freak communion
                              windpools in the ash of palm.

BY LITTLE LOVING

After Thomas Blackburn

By little loving, once, I sought
To conquer pain, a bank of bleached
Shells kept floods at bay – once
By little wisdoms, sought the welcome drought.

By little dreaming, once, I kept
My feet from flowered paths. I bared
The night of stealth, watched thwarted
Winds beat cycles, deafened as a crypt.

The paradox of crowds set a marble wall
Where I fled for keeping. Loneliness feeds
On open faces – once by little seeing, fell
To the still centre, off the ruptured wheel

Of blood. And this, the accident of flesh I hailed
Man's eternal lesson – by little yearning to unwind
Cords of closeness. Enough, I swore, the wear
Of pulses, stretch of flesh hunger hourly howled.

I knew redemption in the truth of hate
Yet, fled the careful balance; once,
By little spending I had built
A hoard of peace, yet wondered at the hurt.

They kept vigil long, the winds and the stilled
Night rage, and the tread of waters proved a lie
Bursting from within . . . once, by little kindling, I
Fell to dying, phoenix of each pyre forestalled.

grey seasons

I THINK IT RAINS

I think it rains
That tongues may loosen from the parch
Uncleave roof-tops of the mouth, hang
Heavy with knowledge

I saw it raise
The sudden cloud, from ashes. Settling
They joined in a ring of grey; within,
The circling spirit

Oh it must rain
These closures on the mind, binding us
In strange despairs, teaching
Purity of sadness

And how it beats
Skeined transparencies on wings
Of our desires, searing dark longings
In cruel baptisms

Rain-reeds, practised in
The grace of yielding, yet unbending
From afar, this your conjugation with my earth
Bares crouching rocks.

PRISONER

Grey, to the low grass cropping
Slung, wet-lichened, wisps from such
Smoke heaviness, elusive of thin blades
Curl inward to the earth, breed
The grey hours,

And days, and years, for do not
The wise grey temples we shall build
To febrile years, here begin – not
In tears and ashes, but on the sad mocking
Threads, compulsive of the hour?

In the desert wildness, when, lone cactus,
Cannibal in his love – even amidst the
Crag and gorge, the leap and night tremors
Even as the potsherd stayed and the sandstorm
Fell – intimations came.

In the whorled centre of the storm, a threnody
But not from this. For that far companion,
Made sudden stranger when the wind slacked
And the centre fell, grief. And the stricken
Potsherd lay, disconsolate – intimations then

But not from these. He knew only
Sudden seizure. And time conquest
Bound him helpless to each grey essence.
Nothing remained if pains and longings
Once, once set the walls; sadness
Closed him, rootless, lacking cause.

SEASON

Rust is ripeness, rust,
And the wilted corn-plume;
Pollen is mating-time when swallows
Weave a dance
Of feathered arrows
Thread corn-stalks in winged
Streaks of light. And, we loved to hear
Spliced phrases of the wind, to hear
Rasps in the field, where corn-leaves
Pierce like bamboo slivers.

Now, garnerers we
Awaiting rust on tassels, draw
Long shadows from the dusk, wreathe
Dry thatch in wood-smoke. Laden stalks
Ride the germ's decay – we await
The promise of the rust.

NIGHT

Your hand is heavy, Night, upon my brow
I bear no heart mercuric like the clouds, to dare
Exarcerbation from your subtle plough.

Woman as a clam, on the far crescent
I saw your jealous eye quench the sea's
Fluorescence, dance on the pulse incessant

Of the waves. And I stood drained
Submitting like the sands, blood and brine
Coursing to the roots. Night, you rained

Serrated shadows through dank leaves
Till, bathed in warm suffusion of your dappled cells
Sensations pained me, faceless, silent night thieves.

Hide me now, when night children haunt the earth –
I must hear none. These misted calls will yet
Undo me, naked, unbidden, at Night's muted birth.

FADO SINGER

For Amalia Roderiguez

My skin is pumiced to a fault
I am down to hair-roots, down to fibre filters
Of the raw tobacco nerve

Your net is spun of sitar strings
To hold the griefs of gods: I wander long
In tear vaults of the sublime

Queen of night torments, you strain
Sutures of song to bear imposition of the rites
Of living and of death. You

Pluck strange dirges from the storm
Sift rare stones from ashes of the moon, and ride
Night errands to the throne of anguish

Oh there is too much crush of petals
For perfume, too heavy tread of air on mothwing
For a cup of rainbow dust

Too much pain, oh midwife at the cry
Of severance, fingers at the cosmic cord, too vast
The pains of easters for a hint of the eternal.

I would be free of your tyranny, free
From sudden plunges of the flesh in earthquake
Beyond all subsidence of sense

I would be free from headlong rides
In rock reams and volcanic veins, drawn by dark steeds
On grey melodic reins.

october '66

IKEJA, FRIDAY, FOUR O'CLOCK

They were but gourds for earth to drink therefrom
The laden trucks, mirage of breath and form

Unbidden offering on the lie of altars
A crop of wrath when hands retract and reason falters

No feast but the eternal retch of human surfeit
No drink but dregs at reckoning of loss and profit

Let nought be wasted, gather up for the recurrent session
Loaves of lead, lusting in the sun's recession.

HARVEST OF HATE

So now the sun moves to die at mid-morning
And laughter wilts on the lips of wine
The fronds of palm are savaged to a bristle
And rashes break on kernelled oil

The hearth is pocked with furnacing of teeth
The air is heavy with rise of incense
For wings womb-moist from the sanctuary of nests
Fall, unfledged to the tribute of fire.

Now pay we forfeit on old abdications
The child dares flames his fathers lit
And in the briefness of too bright flares
Shrivels a heritage of blighted futures

There has been such a crop in time of growing
Such tuneless noises when we longed for sighs
Alone of petals, for muted swell of wine-buds
In August rains, and singing in green spaces.

MASSACRE, OCTOBER '66

Written in Tegel

Shards of sunlight touch me here
Shredded in willows. Through stained-glass
Fragments on the lake I sought to reach
A mind at silt-bed

The lake stayed cold
I swam in an October flush of dying leaves
The gardener's labour flew in seasoned scrolls
Lettering the wind

Swept from painted craft
A mockery of waves remarked this idyll sham
I trod on acorns; each shell's detonation
Aped the skull's uniqueness.

Came sharper reckoning –
This favoured food of hogs cannot number high
As heads still harshly crop to whirlwinds
I have briefly fled

The oak rains a hundred more
A kind confusion to arithmetics of death:
Time to watch autumn the removal man
Dust down rare canvases

To let a loud resolve of passion
Fly to a squirrel, burnished light and copper fur
A distant stance without the lake's churchwindows
And for a stranger, love.

A host of acorns fell, silent
As they are silenced all, whose laughter
Rose from such indifferent paths, oh God
They are not strangers all

Whose desecration mocks the word
Of peace – *salaam aleikun* – not strangers any
Brain of thousands pressed asleep to pig fodder –
Shun pork the unholy – cries the priest.

I borrow seasons of an alien land
In brotherhood of ill, pride of race around me
Strewn in sunlit shards. I borrow alien lands
To stay the season of a mind.

CIVILIAN AND SOLDIER

My apparition rose from the fall of lead,
Declared, 'I'm a civilian.' It only served
To aggravate your fright. For how could I
Have risen, a being of this world, in that hour
Of impartial death! And I thought also: nor is
Your quarrel of this world.

You stood still
For both eternities, and oh I heard the lesson
Of your training sessions, cautioning –
Scorch earth behind you, do not leave
A dubious neutral to the rear. Reiteration
Of my civilian quandry, burrowing earth
From the lead festival of your more eager friends
Worked the worse on your confusion, and when
You brought the gun to bear on me, and death
Twitched me gently in the eye, your plight
And all of you came clear to me.

I hope some day
Intent upon my trade of living, to be checked
In stride by *your* apparition in a trench,
Signalling, I am a soldier. No hesitation then
But I shall shoot you clean and fair
With meat and bread, a gourd of wine
A bunch of breasts from either arm, and that
Lone question – do you friend, even now, know
What it is all about?

FOR FAJUYI

Honour late restored, early ventured to a trial
Of Death's devising. Flare too rare
Too brief, chivalric steel
Redeems us living, springs the lock of Time's denial

Out from miser earth, thrust from dark, a mystery kernel
Latent till the stress of storms
Sudden soared a miracle of boughs
Recreative temper as the sun's, diurnal.

Feet will not record timbres of iron spines –
Pass over: journeys must end.
Home, forgotten is the bridge
Gold dust in the air, sunk the burdened beam of mines

Weeds triumph. Weeds prowl the path of sandals
Thonged to mountains, thonged
To foundries of futures
Kilns fall tepid, bled by feeble candles

Weeds triumph. What goals for pilgrim feet
But to a dearth of wills
To hills and terraces of gods
Echoes for voices, shadows for the lonely feat.

Flowers thronged his feet whose prints were flagstones
Garlands wither, weeds abide
Who seeks breath of him
Tread the span of bridges, look not down to gravestones.

[54]

MALEDICTION

For her who rejoiced

Unsexed, your lips
have framed a life curse
shouting joy where all
the human world
shared in grief's humility.

May this pattern be your life
preserve; that when hearts
are set alive in joy's communion,

a sky of flies in blood-gore
press upon and smear you wholly,

a sky of scab-blacked tears
glut but never slake

those lips
crossed in curse corrugations
thin slit in spittle silting
and bile-blown tongue
pain plagued, a mock man plug
wedged in waste womb-ways
a slime slug slewed in sewage
orogbo egan, gẹgẹ l'ẹkẹ arugbo . . .

Giggles fill the water-hole
Offsprings by you abandoned,
And afterbirth, at crossroads

So when the world grieves, rejoice
Call to them in laughter, beat
Wilted welts on your breasts *bata*
To hyenas of the wastes

even thus
for your children
and your children's
children

that their throats laugh Amen
on your bier, and carousing hooves
raise dust to desecrated dust – Amen.

PREFACE TO *IDANRE*

Idanre was born of two separate halves of the same experience. The first was a visit to the rockhills of that name, a god-suffused grazing of primal giants and mastodons, petrified through some strange history, suckled by mists and clouds. Three years later and some two hundred miles away, a rainstorm rived apart the intervening years and space, leaving a sediment of disquiet which linked me to lingering, unresolved sensations of my first climb up Idanre. I abandoned my work – it was middle of the night – and walked. *Idanre* is the record of that walk through wet woods on the outskirts of Molete, a pilgrimage to Idanre in company of presences such as dilate the head and erase known worlds. We returned at dawn, the sun was rising just below the hut where we had sheltered on the outward journey. The palm wine girl still waited, the only other human being awake in the vast prescient night, yet an eternal presence whose charity had earthed me from the sublimating essence of the night.

There was a final, postscript image. The rainstorm was the first of the season, yet it had the breath of harvest from the first thunderclap. And as the sun rose over a tarmac hill, the year's harvest followed it in extravagant procession, rich, glorious, sensuous with life.

I took my leave of her, my companions had vanished, I returned home wet from overladen boughs, brittle as the herald lightning to a storm. By nightfall that same day, *Idanre* was completed. It has remained much the same over two years, only the occasional change of a word or a line, little more.

Idanre lost its mystification early enough. As events gathered pace and unreason around me I recognised it as part of a pattern of awareness which began when I wrote *A Dance of the Forests*. In detail, in the human context of my society, *Idanre* has made abundant sense. (The town of Idanre itself was the first to cut its bridge, its only link with the rest of the region during the uprising of October '65.) And since then, the bloody origin of Ogun's pilgrimage has been, in true cyclic manner most bloodily re-enacted. Still awaited is that postscript image of dawn, contained even in the beginning, the brief sun-led promise of earth's forgiveness.

IDANRE

Gone, and except for horsemen briefly
Thawed, lit in deep cloud mirrors, lost
The skymen of Void's regenerate Wastes
Striding vast across
My still inchoate earth

The flaming corkscrew etches sharp affinities
(No dream, no vision, no delirium of the dissolute)
When roaring vats of an unstoppered heaven deluge
Earth in fevered distillations, potent with
The fire of the axe-handed one

And greys are violent now, laced with
Whiteburns, tremulous in fire tracings
On detonating peaks. Ogun is still on such
Combatant angles, poised to a fresh descent
Fiery axe-heads fly about his feet

In these white moments of my god, plucking
Light from the day's effacement, the last ember
Glows in his large creative hand, savage round
The rebel mane, ribbed on ridges, crowded in corridors
Low on his spiked symbols

He catches Sango in his three-fingered hand
And runs him down to earth. Safe shields my eaves
This night, I have set the Iron One against
All wayward bolts. Rumours rise on grey corrugations,
The hearth is damped

In gale breaths of the silent blacksmith
Cowls of ashes sweep about his face. Earth
Clutches at the last rallying tendrils
A tongue-tip trembles briefly and withdraws
The last lip of sky is sealed

And no one speaks of secrets in this land
Only, that the skin be bared to welcome rain
And earth prepare, that seeds may swell
And roots take flesh within her, and men
Wake naked into harvest-tide.

II   *. . . and after*

He comes, who scrapes no earthdung from his feet
He comes again in Harvest, the first of reapers
Night is our tryst when sounds are clear
And silences ring pure tones as the pause
Of iron bells

        At pilgrims' rest beneath Idanre Hill
        The wine-girl, dazed from divine dallying
        Felt wine-skeins race in fire-patterns within her
        Her eyes queried, what then are you? At such hour
        Why seek what on the hills?

And she swam an eel into the shadows, felt her limbs
Grow live, the torrents ran within and flooded us
A gourd rose and danced between – without
The night awaited celebration of the crops –
She took, and held it to her womb.

Calm, beyond interpreting, she sat and in her grace
Shared wine with us. The quiet of the night
Shawled us together, secure she was in knowledge
Of that night's benediction. Ogun smiled his peace
Upon her, and we rose

The sky cracked halfways, a greying skull
On blooded highways. I turned, vapours rose
From sodden bitumen and snaked within
Her wrap of indigo, her navel misted over
A sloe bared from the fruit

Darkness veiled her little hills poised
Twin nights against the night, pensive points
In the leer of lightning, and sadness filled
The lone face of the wine-girl; the thatch
Ran rivulets between her breasts.

Harvest night, and time to walk with fruit
Between your lips, on psalming feet. We walked
Silently across a haze of corn, and Ogun
Teased his ears with tassels, his footprints
Future furrows for the giant root

His head was lost among palm towers
And power pylons. Through aeons of darkness rode the stone
Of whirling incandescence, and cables danced
In writhing ecstasies, point to point, wart to wart
Of electric coils

The unit kernel atomised, presaging new cohesions
Forms at metagenesis. Ogun lay on tension wires
Slung in hammock, sail-wing birds of night
Nested in his armpits, through pylon rungs flew
Braids of veins, nerved wings and sonic waves

In the blasting of the seed, in the night-birds'
Instant discernment, in the elemental fusion, seed
To current, shone the godhead essence;
One speeds his captive bolts on filaments
Spun of another's forge. And we

Have honeycombed beneath his hills, worked red earth
Of energies, quarrying rare and urgent ores and paid
With wrecks of last year's suppers, paved his roads
With shells, milestones of breathless bones –
Ogun is a demanding god.

We walked through broken braids of steel
And fallen acrobats. The endless safety nets
Of forests prove a green deception
Fated lives ride on the wheels of death when,
The road waits, famished

Cave and castle, shrine and ghostly grottos
Playthings now of children, shades
For browsing goats. The wheels have fallen
To looters and insurance men, litigant on
Spare part sales and terms of premium

The weeds grow sinuous through gaunt corrosions
Skeletons of speed, earth mounds raised towards
Their seeming exhumation; growth is greener where
Rich blood has spilt; brain and marrow make
Fat manure with sheep's excrement

As the First Boulder, as the errant wheel
Of the death chariot, as the creation snake
Spawned tail in mouth, wind chisels and rain pastes
Rust from steel and bones, wake dormant seeds
And suspended lives. I heard

The silence yield to substance. They rose,
The dead whom fruit and oil await
On doorstep shrine and road, their lips
Moist from the first flakes of harvest rain –
Even gods remember dues.

Ogun, godfather of all souls who by road
Made the voyage home, made his being welcome
Suffused in new powers of night, my skin
Grew light with eyes; I watched them drift away
To join the gathering presences

[65]

Tomorrow they preside, guests unseen
To whom the rams will bow, and with open throats
Quench totemic thirsts, thirst of earth
The hems of hidden voices brush all feet
This night, dew-wet with departed breaths

> *And to the one whose feet were wreathed*
> *In dark vapours from earth's cooling pitch*
> *I earth my being, she who has felt rain's probing*
> *Vines on night's lamp-post, priestess at fresh shrines*
> *Sacred leaf whose hollow gathers rains*

Vast grows the counterpane of nights since innocence
Of apocalyptic skies, when thunderous shields clashed
Across the heights, when bulls leapt cloud humps and
Thunders opened chasms end to end of fire:
The sky a slate of scoured lettering

Of widening wounds eclipsed in smoke, scabbed
From a pale cauterising hand to a jewelled crucifix
Seared in agonic purities. And except
A *certain* knowledge named it the apocalypse, it stayed
Portents in unquiet nights

Where sprang armoured beasts, unidentifiable,
Nozzles of flames, tails of restive gristles
Banners of saints, cavalcades of awesome hosts
Festival of firevales, crush of starlode
And exploding planets

Whorls of intemperate steel, triangles of cabal
In rabid spheres, iron bellows at volcanic tunnels
Easters in convulsions, urged by energies
Of light millenniums, crusades, empires and revolution
Damnations and savage salvations

Later, diminutive zebras raced on track edges
Round the bed, dwarfs blew on royal bugles
A gaunt *ogboni* raised his staff and vaulted on
A zebra's back, galloped up a quivering nose –
A battle with the suffocating shrouds

Opalescent pythons oozed tar coils
Hung from rafters thrashing loops of gelatine
The world was choked in wet embrace
Of serpent spawn, waiting Ajantala's rebel birth
Monster child, wrestling pachyderms of myth,

> *And at the haven of a distant square*
> *Of light, hope's sliver from vile entombment*
> *She waited, caryatid at the door of sanctuary*
> *Her hands were groves of peace, Oya's forehead*
> *Dipped to pools and still hypnotic springs*
>
> *And now she is a dark sheath freed*
> *From Ogun's sword, her head of tapered plaits*
> *A casque of iron filigree, a strength*
> *Among sweet reeds and lemon bushes, palm*
> *And fragrances of rain*

[67]

The night glowed violet about his head
He reached a large hand to tension wires
And plucked a string; earth was a surreal bowl
Of sounds and mystic timbres, his fingers
Drew warring elements to a union of being

And taught the veins to dance, of earth of rock
Of tree, sky, of fire and rain, of flesh of man
And woman. Ogun is the god that ventures first
His path one loop of time, one iron coil
Earth's broken rings were healed

III   *pilgrimage*

We stood upon Idanre's columns and he fell,
The Iron One, to grieving. His breast
The crown of Idanre Hill, stooped, pressed upon
By clouds dark with moulted deeds
And accusing forms

Union they had known until the Boulder
Rolling down the hill of the Beginning
Shred the kernel to a million lights.
A traitor's heart rejoiced, the gods' own slave
Dirt-covered from the deed

Man's passage, pre-ordained, self-ordered winds
In reconstruction. (Piecemeal was *their* deft
Re-birth, a cupped shell of tortoise, staggered
Tile tegument;) And the monolith of man searches still
A blind hunger in the road's hidden belly.

Idanre's boulder complex rose before us and he grieved
The veins were dying in the flesh of earth
Bled of all lustre, the lodes were crumbled
And the fires fallen to ashes. Light, more
Than human frame can bear

Set flanges to a god, control had slipped
Immortal grasp. On the hills of Idanre memories
Grieved him, my Hunter god, Vital
Flint of matter, total essence split again
On recurrent boulders

This road have I trodden in a time beyond
Memory of fallen leaves, beyond
Thread of fossil on the slate, yet I must
This way again. Let all wait the circulation
Of time's acrobat, who pray

For dissolution: the chronicle abides in clay texts
And fossil textures. I followed fearful, archives
Of deities heaved from primal burdens; Ogun
Sought the season's absolution, on the rocks of genesis
Night weighed huge about me

[69]

And I walked in footprints of a god
Whose knees struck sparks to burn the night
Brushing rocks in self-rage up the hill, up
His hermitage in rockshields lost in cloud
Caverns, Outcast Deity!

IV   *the beginning*

Low beneath rockshields, home of the Iron One
The sun had built a fire within
Earth's heartstone. Flames in fever fits
Ran in rock fissures, and hill surfaces
Were all aglow with earth's transparency

      Orisa-nla, Orunmila, Esu, Ifa were all assembled
      Defeated in the quest to fraternise with man

Wordlessly he rose, sought knowledge in the hills
Ogun the lone one saw it all, the secret
Veins of matter, and the circling lodes
Sango's spent thunderbolt served him a hammer-head
His fingers touched earth-core, and it yielded

      To think, a mere plague of finite chaos
      Stood between the gods and man

He made a mesh of elements, from stone
Of fire in earthfruit, the womb of energies
He made an anvil of the peaks, and kneaded
Red clay for his mould. In his hand the Weapon
Gleamed, born of the primal mechanic

      And this pledge he gave the heavens
      I will clear a path to man

His task was ended, he declined the crown
Of deities, sought retreat in heights. But Ire
Laid skilled siege to divine withdrawal. Alas
For diplomatic arts, the Elders of Ire prevailed;
He descended, and they crowned him king

      Who speaks to me in chance recesses
      Who guides the finger's eye

Now he climbs in reparation, who annointed
Godhead in carnage, O let heaven loose the bolts
Of last season's dam for him to lave his fingers
Merely, and in the heady line of blood
Vultures drown. Merely,

And in the lungstreams of depleted pastures
Earth is flattened. O the children of Ogun
Reaped red earth that harvest, rain
Is childrens' reeds and the sky a bird-pond
Until my god has bathed his hands

[71]

Who brings a god to supper, guard him well
And set his place with a long bamboo pole

Ogun is the lascivious god who takes
Seven gourdlets to war. One for gunpowder,
One for charms, two for palm wine and three
Air-sealed in polished bronze make
Storage for his sperms

My god Ogun, orphans' shield, his home
Is terraced hills self-surmounting to the skies
Ogun path-maker, he who goes fore where other gods
Have turned. Shield of orphans, was your shield
In-spiked that day on sheltering lives?

Yet had he fled when his primal task was done
Fugitive from man and god, ever seeking hills
And rock bounds. Idanre's granite offered peace
And there he dwelt until the emissaries came –
Lead us king, and warlord.

Who speaks to me I cannot tell
Who guides the hammer's flight

Gods drowse in boredom, and their pity
Is easy roused with lush obsequious rites
Because the rodent nibbled somewhat at his yam,
The farmer hired a hunter, filled him with wine
And thrust a firebrand in his hand

We do not burn the woods to trap
A squirrel; we do not ask the mountain's
Aid, to crack a walnut.

V   *the battle*

Overtaking fugitives
A rust-red swarm of locusts
Dine off grains

Quick proboscis
Find the coolers
Soon the wells are dry

Presumptuous eaves
Of safety, hang stark
Only this shelter for
Returning men

This filigree
Of foliage veins
Lets in the moon's
Leprous sneer

Truth peeps in
On every side
Welcomes the wind
From frightened men

[73]

Ah but his hands cleave frenetic
To the jig! Prestidigitator god midst head
And limb, they poise a full eternity
And falling, bounce to rare wave-lengths

His sword possesses all

There are air-paths unknown to human sight
Arabesques of light, a keen maze where all
Who seek strategic outlets find
O Iron One

The shortest cut

Storms strain his mighty chest, his nipples
Glow with blackness, from hair-roots
Spit black jets of flames. Tall he rises to the hills
His head a rain-cloud has eclipsed the sun
His nostrils blow visible

Exhalations as twin-flues through clouds
There are myriad lesser motes in flight
And leaping mists. Never to his ears,
Never to him comes the cry of men
In sweet lather of death.

Lord of all witches, divine hunter
Your men Ogun, your men!

[74]

His sword an outer crescent of the sun
No eye can follow it, no breath draws
In wake of burning vapour. Still they cry

Your men Ogun! Your men!

This blade he forged, its progress
Never falters, rivulets on it so swift
The blood forgets to clot

There are falling ears of corn
And ripe melons tumble from the heads
Of noisy women, crying

Lust-blind god, gore-drunk Hunter
Monster deity, you destroy your men!

He strides sweat encrusted
Bristles on risen tendons
Porcupine and barbed. Again he turns
Into his men, a butcher's axe
Rises and sinks

Behind it, a guest no one
Can recall.

Where do we seek him, they asked?
Where conflcit rages, where sweat
Is torrents of rain, where clear springs
Of blood fill one with longing
As the rush of wine

[75]

So there they sought
And there they find him

And youth that came to teeth on the encounter?
What greater boon for the fledgeling! The wings
Of a god enclose him wholly, there is
No room for air

        Smothered in wind-deafness
        Blinded in light-paths of suns

There are air-beams unfelt by human breath
Unseen by sight, intangible. Whose throat
Draws breath in a god's preserve
Breathes the heart of fire

        Murderer, stay your iron hand
        Your men lie slain – Cannibal!

Ay, ring summons on the deafened god
His fingers sow red earth. His being incarnate
Bathes in carnage, anoints godhead
In carnage

To bring a god to supper is devout, yet
A wise host keeps his distance till
The Spirit One has dined his fill. What mortal
Brands a platter with an awesome name,
Or feeds him morsels choice without
Gauntlets of iron. A human feast
Is indifferent morsel to a god.

[76]

A lethal arc
Completes full circle

Unsheathed
The other half
Of fire

Incinerates
All subterfuge
Enthrones
The fatal variant

The rodent's nose explored the shadows
Found sweat and gangrene
Smell the same to a skin tailor. Beyond
A prayer for sunshine, what interest
Does a stagnant pool pretend
To a river in flood?

The rams
Are gathered to the stream
For blessing

Hour of prayer
And curved horns curve
Into hearts of the faithful

The priest
Cleansed his fingers
In new springs

[77]

And drank.
All routes led
To the sacrificial knife

That dawn
On the plains of prayer
A flat stream
And new springs

All prayers were one
To the Iron One

Let each seek wisdom where he can, life's
Puppetry creaks round me hourly
Trunks and motions in masquerade grotesques
Post-mortem is for quacks and chroniclers
Who failed at divination

Esu, my little prince of games sat
On his head, and he was deaf to identifying
Cries. Too late came warning that a god
Is still a god to men, and men are one
When knowledge comes, of death.

And they were cast adrift, without
Direction for new prayers, their cry
For partial succour brought a total hand
That smothered life on crimson plains
With too much answering

The royal baobab
Dances with the head alone
To a wind's possession

    Who has no roots
    In earth
    Deep in rock-chambers . . .

Its eardrops
Makes a wine-cup
Of my sheltering head

When the wind insists

    Who has no root
    In earth
    Flee the shelter
    Of a god possessed

Light filled me then, intruder though
I watched a god's excorsis; clearly
The blasphemy of my humanity rose accusatory
In my ears, and understanding came
Of a fatal condemnation

And in that moment broke his crust of separation
And the blood-scales of his eyes. A wind's insinuation
Lowered his arm, scattering blood-fogs; revealed
The vessel that was singly cast, crepitate
In orphan sherds.

He recognised the pattern of the spinning rock
And Passion slowly yielded to remorse

Melted then the wine-logged eyes, embers
No gourd ever assuaged, kernels fire-red
On blacksmith tongs. A god knows no comforter
And I am not prone to pity. Divine outcast
And your captains bold?

Did not your primal science reave discs
Of light, a keen maze for pupils of the forge?

Too late for joy, the Hunter stayed his hand
The chute of truth opened from red furnaces
And Ogun stayed his hand

Truth, a late dawn,

Life, the two-cowrie change of the dealer
In trinkets lay about him in broken threads
Oh the squirrel ran up an *iroko* tree
And the hunter's chase
Was ended.

I walked upon a deserted night before
The gathering of Harvest, companion at a god's
Pre-banquet. The hills of Idanre beckoned me
As who would yield her secrets, locked
In sepulchral granite.

Sightless eyes prayed haste upon
His slow descent, incurious to behold
The claws of day rip wide the weakened shutters
Of a mind divine. Who knows from what savage
Tumours, floods a god's remorse.

A child averts his eye from an elder's
Nakedness; pursued by blood in his lone descent
The silence said, Go your way, and if
Our dead pass you on your way, smooth their path
To where is home.

He who had sought heights inaccessible to safeguard
The vital flint, heard, not voices whom the hour
Of death had made all one, nor futile flight
But the assertive act of Atunda, and he was shamed
In recognition of the grim particular

It will be time enough, and space, when we are dead
To be a spoonful of the protoplasmic broth
Cold in wind-tunnels, lava flow of nether worlds
Deaf to thunder blind to light, comatose
In one omni-sentient cauldron

Time enough to abdicate to astral tidiness
The all in one, superior annihilation of the poet's
Diversity – oh how his words condemn him, who declared
A fragrance in the stars, plunged to the mind's abyss
In contemplation of a desert well

I shall remain in knowledge of myself, as Idanre's
Bold concretion at the night, wear its anonymity
Not dissolution. For who will stand beside
The god, who welcome rain, who celebrate Idanre
Iterate carbuncle of Night?

Who, inhesion of disparate senses, of matter
Thought, entities and motions, who sleep-walk
Incensed in Nirvana – a code of Passage
And the Night – who, cloyed, a mote in homogeneous gel
Touch the living and the dead?

Rather, may we celebrate the stray electron, defiant
Of patterns, celebrate the splitting of the gods
Cannonisation of the strong hand of a slave who set
The rock in revolution – and the Boulder cannot
Up the hill in time's unwind.

You who have borne the first separation, bide you
Severed still; he who guards the Creative Flint
Walks, purged spirit, contemptuous of womb-yearnings
He shall teach us to ignite our several kilns
And glory in each bronzed emergence.

[82]

All hail Saint Atunda, First revolutionary
Grand iconoclast at genesis – and the rest in logic
Zeus, Osiris, Jahweh, Christ in trifoliate
Pact with creation, and the wisdom of Orunmila, Ifa
Divining eyes, multiform

Evolution of the self-devouring snake to spatials
New in symbol, banked loop of the 'Mobius Strip'
And interlock of re-creative rings, one surface
Yet full comb of angles, uni-plane, yet sensuous with
Complexities of mind and motion.

VII   *harvest*

Night sets me free; I suffer skies to sprout
Ebb to full navel in progressive arcs, ocean
Of a million roe, highway of eyes and moth-wings.
Night sets me free, I ride on ovary silences
In the wake of ghosts

Ogun's mantle brushed the leaves, the phase of night
Was mellow wine joined to a dirge
Of shadows, the air withdrew to scything motions
Of his dark-shod feet, seven-ply crossroads
Hands of camwood, breath of indigo

[83]

Night sets me free, soft sediments on skin
And sub-soil mind . . . Dawn came gradual, mists
Fell away from rock and honeycomb, Idanre woke
To braided vapours, a dance of seven veils
The septuple god was groom and king.

Mists fell to mote infinities from mountain face
Retrieved, were finely gathered to a sponge
Of froth murmurs in palm veins, he rinsed
The sunrise of his throat in agile wine; I took the sun
In his copper calabash

Dawn, He who had dire reaped
And in wrong season, bade the forests swallow him
And left mankind to harvest. At pilgrim lodge
The wine-girl kept lone vigil, fused still
In her hour of charity

A dawn of bright processions, the sun peacocked
Loud, a new mint of coins. And those were all
The night hours, only the dissipated gourds,
Rain serried floor, fibre walls in parsimonious
Sifting of the sun, and she . . .

Light burnished to a copper earth, cornucopia
Fell in light cascades round her feet. Our paths
Grew solemn as her indrawn eye, bride of Night
Hoard of virgin dawns, expectant grew her distant gaze
And Harvest came, responsive

The first fruits rose from subterranean hoards
First in our vision, corn sheaves rose over hill
Long before the bearers, domes of eggs and flesh
Of palm fruit, red, oil black, froth flew in sun bubbles
Burst over throngs of golden gourds

And they moved towards resorption in His alloy essence
Primed to a fusion, primed to the sun's dispersion
Containment and communion, seed-time and harvest, palm
And pylon, Ogun's road a 'Mobius' orbit, kernel
And electrons, wine to alchemy.

I *deluge . . .*

   1. axe-handed one   Sango, god of lightning and electricity.

   2. Ogun   God of Iron and metallurgy, Explorer, Artisan, Hunter, God of war, Guardian of the Road, the Creative Essence. His season is harvest and the rains.

   3. Sango   See 1 above.

II *. . . and after*

   1. wine-girl   Also Oya, once the wife of Ogun, latterly of Sango. (Worn out by Ogun's fearsome nature, she deserted him for Sango). Also a dead girl, killed in a motor accident.

   2. etc.   This and following stanzas celebrate the fusion of the two essences, Ogun and Sango, already symbolised in the person of their common wife, Oya. Today Ogun of the metallic lore conducts Sango's electricity. The ritual dance of the union is seen sometimes during an electric storm when from high-tension wires leap figures of ecstatic flames. This is the ideal fusion – to preserve the original uniqueness and yet absorb another essence.

   3. etc.   Apocalyptic visions of childhood and other deliriums.

   4. ogboni   Cultic executive of Yoruba society; an elders' conclave, a member.

[86]

5. Ajantala	Archetype of the rebel child, iconoclast, anarchic, anti-clan, anti-matriarch, virile essence in opposition to womb-domination.
III *the pilgrimage*	
1. traitor	Atoǫda (also called Atunda), slave to first deity. Either from pique or revolutionary ideas he rolled a rock down onto his unsuspecting master, smashing him to bits and creating the multiple godhead.
IV *in the beginning*	
1. Orisa-nla	Head of the deities.
Orunmila	Sky-god, essence of wisdom
Esu	God of chance, disruption.
Ifa	Divination and order.
V *the battle*	
	Ogun's day of error. King of Ire against his will, he soon led his men into battle. Drunk with wine and blinded by gore Ogun turned on his own men and slaughtered them. Annually he re-enacts his deed of shame.
VI *recessional*	
1. Atoǫda	See III, 1.
2. Mobius Strip	A mathe-magical ring, infinite in self-recreation into independent but linked rings and therefore the freest conceivable (to me) symbol of human or divine (e.g. Yoruba, Olympian) relationships. A symbol of optimism also, as it gives the illusion of a 'kink' in the circle

and a possible centrifugal escape from the eternal cycle of karmas that has become the evil history of man. Only an illusion but a poetic one, for the Mobius strip is a very simple figure of aesthetic and scientific truths and contradictions. In this sense, it is the symbol of Ogun in particular, and an evolution from the tail-devouring snake which he sometimes hangs around his neck and symbolizes the doom of repetition. And even if the primal cycle were of good and innocence, the Atoóda of the world deserve praise for introducing the evolutionary 'kink'.

VII *harvest*

1. alchemy

The magic communion of the body, the earth and metals (see Camara Laye's account of his goldsmith father at work). Blood tempers steel, and so may wine.